It's True:
Our God Resurrects

Alyssa Kruschke

WestBow Press books may be ordered through booksellers or by contacting:

WestBow Press
A Division of Thomas Nelson & Zondervan
1663 Liberty Drive
Bloomington, IN 47403
www.westbowpress.com
844-714-3454

ISBN: 978-1-6642-6100-6 (sc)
ISBN: 978-1-6642-6053-5 (hc)
ISBN: 978-1-6642-6054-2 (e)

Library of Congress Control Number: 2022904983

Print information available on the last page.

WestBow Press rev. date: 03/29/2022

WESTBOW
PRESS®
A DIVISION OF THOMAS NELSON
& ZONDERVAN

It's True: Our God Resurrects!

When something dies, we think that's the end. But when it comes to our God, that just isn't true! Our God is more powerful than *death*. Our God performs miracles that we can't even understand, that we couldn't have asked for because we never would've thought they were possible.

But… the cool thing is, that's our God. God's work *is* miracles. God takes what is dead and effortlessly brings it to life. And Jesus wasn't the only person God raised from the dead. Not even close! God brings things back to life all the time.

It's true! Ask Jairus' daughter. Jesus held her hand, spoke to her, and brought her back to life. That's how powerful He is! He only had to touch her and speak, and she went from dead to living.

Mark 5:22-24, 35-36, 38-42 (GNT) "Jairus, an official of the local synagogue, arrived, and when he saw Jesus, he threw himself down at his feet and begged him earnestly, 'My little daughter is very sick. Please come and place your hands on her, so that she will get well and live!' Then Jesus started off with him. So many people were going along with Jesus that they were crowding him from every side... Some messengers came from Jairus' house and told him, 'Your daughter has died. Why bother the Teacher any longer?' Jesus paid no attention to what they said, but told him, 'Don't be afraid, only believe.' They arrived at Jairus' house, where Jesus saw the confusion and heard all the loud crying and wailing. He went in and said to them, 'Why all this confusion? Why are you crying? The child is not dead – she is only sleeping!' They started making fun of him, so he put them all out, took the child's father and mother and his three disciples, and went into the room where the child was lying. He took her by the hand and said to her, 'Talitha, koum,' which means, 'Little girl, I tell you to get up!' She got up at once and started walking around. (She was twelve years old.) When this happened, they were completely amazed."

It's true! Ask the boy who was dead in his coffin. Jesus touched the coffin and spoke to the boy. He sat up - in his coffin - and came back to life. Imagine seeing, with your own eyes, someone popping up out of their coffin! Our God is amazing! Again, with just a touch and His voice, He brought the dead to life.

Luke 7:11-17 (ERV) "The next day Jesus and his followers went to a town called Nain. A big crowd was traveling with them. When Jesus came near the town gate, he saw some people carrying a dead body. It was the only son of a woman who was a widow. Walking with her were many other people from town. When the Lord saw the woman, he felt sorry for her and said, 'Don't cry.' He walked to the open coffin and touched it. The men who were carrying the coffin stopped. Jesus spoke to the dead son: 'Young man, I tell you, get up!' Then the boy sat up and began to talk, and Jesus gave him back to his mother."

It's true! Ask Jesus' friend Lazarus. People, especially Lazarus' sisters, were hurt that Jesus hadn't gotten there in time to save Lazarus because they knew that Lazarus and Jesus were good friends. But Jesus had a miracle in mind for his friend. Lazarus' sisters didn't want to open the tomb because Lazarus had already been dead for four days. Stinky! Gross!

But Jesus insisted.

Jesus prayed and then called Lazarus out. Lazarus, who had been dead 4 days, walked out, all wrapped up in his grave clothes. He was just the same old Lazarus, back to life - healed completely.

Luke 11: 1, 3-5, 17, 20-29, 32-44 (ERV) "There was a man named Lazarus who was sick. So Mary and Martha sent someone to tell Jesus, 'Lord, your dear friend Lazarus is sick.' When Jesus heard this he said, 'The end of this sickness will not be death. No, this sickness is for the glory of God. This has happened to bring glory to the Son of God.' Jesus loved Martha and her sister and Lazarus. Jesus arrived in Bethany and found that Lazarus had already been dead and in the tomb for four days. When Martha heard that Jesus was coming, she went out to greet him. But Mary stayed home. Martha said to Jesus, 'Lord, if you had been here, my brother would not have died. But I know that even now God will give you anything you ask.' Jesus said, 'Your brother will rise and be alive again.' Martha answered, 'I know that he will rise to live again at the time of the resurrection on the last day.' Jesus said to her, 'I am the resurrection. I am the life. Everyone who believes in me will have life, even if they die. And everyone who lives and believes in me will never really die. Martha, do you believe this?' Martha answered, 'Yes, Lord. I believe that you are the Messiah, the Son of God. You are the one who was coming to the world.' After Martha said these things, she went back to her sister Mary. She talked to Mary alone and said, 'The Teacher is here. He is asking for you.' When Mary heard this, she stood up and went quickly to Jesus. When she saw him, she bowed at his feet and said, 'Lord, if you had been here, my brother would not have died.' When Jesus saw Mary crying and the people with her crying too, he was very upset and deeply troubled. He asked, 'Where did you put him?' They said, 'Lord, come and see.' Jesus cried. And the Jews said, 'Look! He loved Lazarus very much!' But some of them said, 'Jesus healed the eyes of the blind man. Why didn't he help Lazarus and stop him from dying?' Again feeling very upset, Jesus came to the tomb. It was a cave with a large stone covering the entrance. He said, "Move the stone away.' Martha said, 'But, Lord, it has been four days since Lararus died. There will be a bad smell.' Then Jesus said to her, 'Remember what I told you? I said that if you believed, you would see God's divine greatness.' So they moved the stone away from the entrance. Then Jesus looked up and said, 'Father, I thank you that you heard me. I know that you always hear me. But I said these things because of the people here around me. I want them to believe that you sent me.' After Jesus said this he called in a loud voice, 'Lazarus, come out!' The dead man came out. His hands and feet were wrapped with pieces of cloth. He had a handkerchief covering his face. Jesus said to the people, 'Take off the cloth and let him go.'

After Jesus died, people doubted that he would rise from the dead. Even though he had brought others back to life. Even though he had told his disciples that this would happen. Even though 700 YEARS earlier, the Bible had promised His Son would come to die to save His people. People. Still. Doubted. Because it seems impossible. But...

It's true! Ask the empty tomb. Jesus' grave was empty. He was risen! He was risen, indeed!

Matthew 28: 1-6 (ERV) "The day after the Sabbath day was the first day of the week. That day at dawn Mary Magdalene and the other woman named Mary went to look at the tomb. Suddenly an angel of the Lord came from the sky, and there was a huge earthquake. The angel went to the tomb and rolled the stone away from the entrance. Then he sat on top of the stone. The angel was shining as bright as lightning. His clothes were as white as snow. The soldiers guarding the tomb were very afraid of the angel. They shook with fear and then became like dead men. The angel said to the women, "Don't be afraid. I know you are looking for Jesus, the one who was killed on the cross. But he is not here. He has risen from death, as he said he would. Come and see where his body was."'

Even some of Jesus' disciples doubted that he could come back to life. I get it, it seems impossible, but come on! They should've known that God can do anything; they got to see Jesus heal and save, miracle after miracle! But they had to *see* to believe that it was true!

It's true! Ask his friends who got to see him again, face-to-face, **after** they watched him die and be buried.

Matthew 28:8-9 (ERV) "So the women hurried from the tomb, afraid yet filled with joy, and ran to tell his disciples. Suddenly Jesus met them. 'Greetings,' he said. They came to him, clasped his feet and worshipped him."

John 20:19-20 (NLT) "That Sunday evening the disciples were meeting behind locked doors because they were afraid of the Jewish leaders. Suddenly, Jesus was standing there among them! 'Peace be with you,' he said. As he spoke, he showed them the wounds in his hands and his side. They were filled with joy when they saw the Lord!"

John 20:24-28 (NLT) "One of the twelve disciples, Thomas (nicknamed the Twin), was not with the others when Jesus came. They told him, 'We have seen the Lord!' But he replied, 'I won't believe it unless I see the nail wounds in his hands, put my fingers into them, and place my hand into the wound in his side.' Eight days later the disciples were together again, and this time Thomas was with them. The doors were locked; but suddenly, as before, Jesus was standing among them. 'Peace be with you,' he said. Then he said to Thomas, 'Put your finger here, and look at my hands. Put your hand into the wound in my side. Don't be faithless any longer. Believe!' 'My Lord and my God!' Thomas exclaimed.

Before Jesus died, He told His disciples that after He died they would have the ability to perform miracles like Jesus had been doing! He said, "I am telling you the truth: those who believe in me will do what I do - yes, they will do even greater things, because I am going to the Father. And I will do whatever you ask for in my name, so that the Father's glory will be shown through the Son." (John 14:12-13, GNT)

Wait...what? Even greater things? Greater things than the guy who gave sight to the blind? Made the lame walk? Healed leprosy? And RAISED PEOPLE FROM THE DEAD?

It's true! Ask Peter what he was able to do! He went to the home of a woman who had already died, her body was ready to be buried. He went into her room, *prayed*, and then told her to get up. He told a dead body to get up. What do you think other people thought of that?

But guess what? But she did! The dead woman got up!

Peter was able to bring her back to life, in Jesus' name, so that others would be able to see God's power and believe in him, just like Jesus promised.

Acts 9:36-42 (GNT) In Joppa there was a woman named Tabitha, who was a believer. (Her name in Greek is Dorcas, meaning "a deer.") She spent all her time doing good and helping the poor. At that time she got sick and died. Her body was washed and laid in a room upstairs. Joppa was not very far from Lydda, and when the believers in Joppa heard that Peter was in Lydda, they sent two men to him with the message, "Please hurry and come to us." So Peter got ready and went with them. When he arrived, he was taken to the room upstairs, where all the widows crowded around him, crying and showing him all the shirts and coats that Dorcas had made while she was alive. Peter put them all out of the room, and he knelt down and prayed; then he turned to the body and said, "Tabitha, get up!" She opened her eyes, and when she saw Peter, she sat up. Peter reached over and helped her get up. Then he called all the believers, including the widows, and presented her alive to them. The news about this spread all over Joppa, and many people believed in the Lord."

Imagine seeing these miracles for yourself. Being there to watch a boy sit up in his coffin. Watching Lazarus walk out of his grave 4 days after being buried. Meeting the angel at Jesus's grave. Meeting Jesus after you watched him die on the cross.

Guess what... God has miracles for *you*, too! Proof, right in front of your very eyes, that He is still taking dead things and bringing them to life.

Go outside. Look closely. We see *so* many things in nature that go from dead to life over and over again. God does that! God gives things in nature their own, unique ways of surviving - surviving extreme heat, extreme cold, even surviving death.

It's true! Ask the maple tree. In Fall, these breath-taking orange, yellow, or red leaves drop from the tree, leaving it bare. Dead. Covered in snow and ice throughout the winter. But when spring comes, the inside of the tree thaws, sap runs out, giving us a resurrection bonus - maple syrup! Buds reappear and the tree produces new leaves to replace the ones it lost. The green leaves brighten our view as we welcome spring. God brings these trees to life over, and over, and over again. God can do this hundreds of times, year after year!

It's true! Ask the flowers. Flowers don't thrive in cold, snowy winters. So, as the temperatures drop, perennial flowers will send their nutrients down, out of their leaves and stems, into their roots for the winter. The rest of the plant dies. Many flowers are cut down to the ground. No more eye-catching colors in our flower beds. Just brown. Dead. Bare.

Flower beds sit, colorless, cut down, empty. For months. But when spring comes, these flowers re-grow from just their roots. That's all they need. Once again, flower beds overflow with an abundance of color. Taking our breath away as they bring life to the front of our homes.

It's true! Ask the bat. When bats hibernate they can breathe only 12 times - a DAY! Their hearts go from beating 1,000 times a minute to about 25 times a minute. Not much happening. Just hanging upside-down, waiting. But when spring comes and it warms up, God brings their bodies back to life. They come out and get to work, catching up to 1,000 mosquitos in just one hour!

It's true! Ask the snail. God gave snails a safe place to hide from the cold, right on their own backs. Yep, their shells! And God made them so they can seal up in their shells and survive without food for years if they need to. Like the others, when temperatures rise and their bodies are able to survive, God will bring them back to life.

It's true! Ask the wood frog. His heart LITERALLY STOPS beating. He stops breathing COMPLETELY. I would call that dead, wouldn't you? He can freeze solid. But when he thaws out, that heart pumps, and he breathes again. God brings him back to life. Year after year! And that might be happening right in your backyard!

It's true! Ask the woolly bear caterpillar. These busy caterpillars are easy to find in Fall as they scurry around, looking for a bed of leaves or a rotting log to protect them during their hibernation. God gave their bodies the ability to freeze solid during the winter months. You can't do that! But these little guys can! They can shut their bodies down, like turning themselves "off". But when their bodies thaw, they are "on" again. They'll eat for just a couple of days before creating a cocoon. Once again, they require no food or water as they somehow, by another absolute phenomenon, transform into the Isabella Tiger Moth.

Freezing solid. Shutting down and then coming back to life. Spinning a cocoon. Morphing into another living thing. These little caterpillars are *way* cooler than we give them credit for.

It's true! Ask the lungfish. God gave lungfish the ability to breathe like other fish, with gills, but he also gave them lungs. They can breathe air! So, when their homes suffer droughts and they have no water, these fish just breathe air. But that's not all! Next, they dig down in the mud and God gives them special mucus that they can cover themselves with to keep them from drying out. They can stay underground for up to *4 years* and still come back to life when the rains come back and the droughts are over. God made them so special, so tough, that lungfish have been alive since *before the dinosaurs*. Whatever killed the dinosaurs, yes, like T-Rex and his buddies, did NOT kill them. They're still alive today!

But what about when we can't see it with our own eyes? Is God still working if we can't see it? Of course He is!

It's true! Ask God about that special someone you loved and treasured who has died. Jesus has promised to bring them back to life. And it's not too hard for him.

1 Thessalonians 4:13-14 (NLT) "And now, dear brothers and sisters, we want you to know what will happen to the believers who have died so you will not grieve like people who have no hope. For since we believe that Jesus died and was raised to life again, we also believe that when Jesus returns, God will bring back with him the believers who have died."

It's true for you! You have nothing to fear. We can see that He is able to do it. Our God resurrects! And He has promised to do it for you. And me.

1 Corinthians 6:14 (NIV) *"By his power God raised the Lord from the dead, and he will raise us also."*

Isaiah 25:8 (ERV) *"But death will be destroyed forever. And the Lord GOD will wipe away every tear from every face. In the past, all of his people were sad, but God will take away that sadness from the earth. All of this will happen because the Lord said it would."*

Jesus said John 6:40 (GNT) *"For what my Father wants is that all who see the Son and believe in him should have eternal life. And I will raise them to life on the last day."*

John 11:25 (NLT) *"Jesus told her, 'I am the resurrection and the life. Anyone who believes in me will live, even after dying.'"*

John 10:28 (GNT) *"I give them eternal life, and they shall never die. No one can snatch them away from me."*

After he raises us, God has plans beyond our imaginations for us. Eternal life is going to be perfect. And Jesus died so that YOU could be there. Because he loves you and he has always wanted you to enjoy your life in a perfect paradise with him.

Job 19: 25, 27 (ERV) "I know that there is someone to defend me and that he lives! And in the end, he will stand here on earth and defend me. I will see him with my own eyes. I myself, not someone else, will see God. And I cannot tell you how excited that makes me feel."

Isaiah 11:6-9 (GNT) "Wolves and sheep will live together in peace, and leopards will lie down with young goats. Calves and lion cubs will feed together, and little children will take care of them. Cows and bears will eat together, and their calves and cubs will lie down in peace. Lions will eat straw as cattle do. Even a baby will not be harmed if it plays near a poisonous snake. On Zion, God's sacred hill, there will be nothing harmful or evil. The land will be as full of knowledge of the Lord as the seas are full of water."

Revelation 21:3-5 (GNT) "I heard a loud voice speaking from the throne: 'Now God's home is with people! He will live with them, and they shall be his people. God himself will be with them, and he will be their God. He will wipe away all tears from their eyes. There will be no more death, no more grief or crying or pain. The old things have disappeared.' Then the one who sits on the throne said, 'And now I make all things new!'"

God and Jesus are always working to bring things to new life. Look around you! And remember that God can resurrect! It sounds insane! Bonkers! Nuts! But God can do it! He does it all the time. Even when we can't understand it. That's who our God is. He's a God of miracles. It's true - Our God resurrects! Let's celebrate that!

"Jesus looked at them and said, 'WIth man this is impossible, but with God all things are possible.'"
Matthew 19:26 (NIV)

Reader's Guide

Why didn't Jesus go save Lazarus before he died if he loved him so much?

If God didn't keep the person you loved from dying, does that mean he didn't love that person? Or that he doesn't care about you and others who are sad, missing that person? Look at how Jesus felt for Jairus, the mother of the boy, Lazarus and his sisters.

What things that can be brought back to life in nature are the most amazing to you? What other things can you think of that die and then come back to life over and over again?

Draw what heaven looks like in your mind. Who is there? How do the people feel and look? Are there animals? How is it different from the world we live in today?

Lots of people doubted Jesus - doubted that he could help Jairus' daughter, that he could help Lazarus, that he himself could come back to life. Do you think Jesus was mad at the people who doubted? How does Jesus respond to people who doubt? How do you think he responds to our doubts and questions?

How can we be confident that God can resurrect?

Afterword

I can't thank God enough for calling me to this. It's a dream come true to create something with Him that I can share with my children. Something that reveals who our God is. Something that draws us into His Presence. That's my heart. Working everyday to know who He is, to spend time looking at what He's done by reading His Word, to see what He does in nature, and to thank Him for all He's doing in my life. Growing to know Him, to trust Him more, to walk with Him. It is my prayer that all readers, adults and children, walk away with something life-giving that opens your eyes and draws you to Him. Calling you to spend more time enjoying our God and celebrating who He is, what He can do, what He does, and what He has promised.

Printed in the United States
by Baker & Taylor Publisher Services